Famous Paintings
Adult Coloring Book

Light Grayscale Edition
For Colored Pencils and Other Coloring Mediums

Sheila Dunn

Printed by CreateSpace, an Amazon.com company
Available at Amazon.com and other online retailers

Special thanks to The Athenaeum website, www.the-athenaeum.org
for providing the color photographs included in this book.

For more information about Sheila Dunn's coloring books and artwork,
please visit her Artist Facebook page at www.facebook.com/Artist4Christ

About this Book

Coloring masterpieces from history is not only relaxing but wonderful practice for using color and rendering light and shadow. This book contains a sample of famous paintings selected from art history. The original painting in full color is shown on the left to provide an easy reference. However, no one should feel forced to follow the example of the original artist. Feel free to use any colors you choose.

I hope you enjoy this collection. To see original art by Sheila Dunn, please visit her Facebook artist page at www.facebook.com/Artist4Christ. On her Facebook page, you can see the latest releases of coloring books as well as what is happening in her art studio.

The Arnolfini Wedding (1434), Jan van Eyck

Mona Lisa (c. 1503-1505), Leonardo da Vinci

St. George and the Dragon (1505-1506), Raphael

Christ with Martha and Mary (1570), Jacopo Tintoretto

The Lute Player (1596), Caravaggio

The Virgin and Child with St. Martina and St. Agnes (1597-1599), El Greco

The Adoration of the Magi (1624), Peter Paul Rubens

Las Meninas (The Maids of Honor) (1656-1657), Diego Velázquez

Girl with a Pearl Earring (1665-1666), Johannes Vermeer

The Harvest (1786-1787), Francisco Jose de Goya y Lucientes

Napoleon Crossing the Alps (1805), Jacques-Louis David

The Great Wave off Kanagawa (c. 1830), Katsushika Hokusai

Whistler's Mother (1871), James Abbott McNeill Whistler

Apples and Biscuits (1880), Paul Cézanne

On Stage (1879-1881), Edgar Degas

A Bar at the Folies-Bergere (1882), Edouard Manet

The Café Terrace on the Place de Forum, Arles, At Night (1888)
Vincent van Gogh

Eiffel Tower (1889), Georges Seurat

The Beginning of the Quadrille at the Moulin Rouge (1892), Henri de Toulouse-Lautrec

Girls at the Piano (1892), Pierre Auguste Renoir

Matamoe (1892), Paul Gauguin

The Child's Bath (c.1893), Mary Cassatt

Water-lilies (1907), Claude Monet

Claude Monet 1907

The Kiss (1907-1908), Gustav Klimt

Jeanne Hebuterne (1919), Amedeo Modigliani

For more coloring fun, please check out the other coloring books by Sheila Dunn including:

Art Coloring Book for Adults: Vincent van Gogh

Art Coloring Book for Adults: Edgar Degas

Dangles and Gems

Love and Lighthouses

Bible Verses of Hope

www.ingramcontent.com/pod-product-compliance
Lightning Source LLC
Chambersburg PA
CBHW050811180526
45159CB00004B/1632